DOLPHINS

WHITE-SIDED DOLPHINS

JOHN F. PREVOST

ABDO & Daughters

Published by Abdo & Daughters, 4940 Viking Drive, Suite 622, Edina, Minnesota 55435.

Library bound edition distributed by Rockbottom Books, Pentagon Tower, P.O. Box 36036, Minneapolis, Minnesota 55435.

Printed in the United States.

Cover Photo credit: Peter Arnold, Inc.
Interior Photo credits: Peter Arnold, Inc. pages 5, 7, 11, 13, 15, 17 ,19
Animals Animals, page 9.

Edited by Bob Italia

Library of Congress Cataloging-in-Publication Data

Prevost, John F.
  White-sided dolphin / John F. Prevost.
    p. cm. — (Dolphins)
Includes bibliographical references (p.23) and index.
ISBN 1-56239-494-0
1. Atlantic white-sided dolphin—Juvenile literature. 2. Pacific whitesided dolphin—Juvenile literature. [1. Atlantic white-slded dolphin. 2. Pacific whitesided
dolphin. 3. Dolphins.] I. Title. II . Series: Prevost, John F. Dolphins.
QL737.C432P746   1995
599.5'3—dc20   95-8121
                                    CIP
                                                                        AC

ABOUT THE AUTHOR

John Prevost is a marine biologist and diver who has been active in conservation and education issues for the past 18 years. Currently he is living inland and remains actively involved in freshwater and marine husbandry, conservation and education projects.

Contents

WHITE-SIDED DOLPHINS AND FAMILY

White-sided dolphins live in the northern waters of the Atlantic and Pacific oceans. Dolphins are small-toothed whales. Whales are **mammals**. They have some hair when born, are **warm blooded**, and make milk for their babies. They are called white-sided because of the light stripe on each side of their body.

There are 2 different **species** of white-sided dolphins: Atlantic white-sided dolphins and Pacific white-sided dolphins. Other group members are the white-beaked, dusky, hourglass, Peale's, and Fraser's dolphins.

White-sided dolphins live in the northern waters of the Atlantic and Pacific oceans.

SIZE, SHAPE AND COLOR

Atlantic white-sided dolphins may reach 9 feet (2.7 meters) in length. The Pacific white-sided dolphin is smaller and may reach 7.5 feet (2.3 meters) in length. The females of both **species** are slightly smaller than the males.

White-sided dolphins have streamlined bodies and a short **snout**. The **flippers** are long and curved. The **dorsal** fin is tall and triangle-shaped.

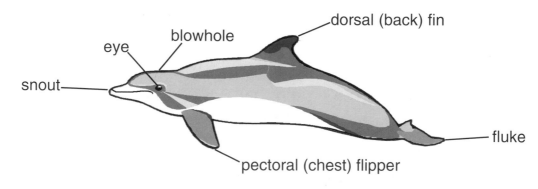

Most dolphins share the same features.

White-sided dolphins have streamlined bodies and short snouts.

White-sided dolphins are marked with different bands of color. The upper part of the body is black or dark gray. The underside is white or light gray. The sides have bands of white and gray. The Atlantic white-sided dolphin has a tan or yellowish stripe starting behind the **dorsal** fin and extending almost to the **flukes**.

WHERE THEY LIVE

White-sided dolphins are found in the **temperate** and **sub-polar** waters of the North Atlantic, and in the temperate waters of the North Pacific. They are often seen riding the **bow waves** of large ships.

The Atlantic white-sided dolphins range from Massachusetts to Greenland, Iceland, Norway and

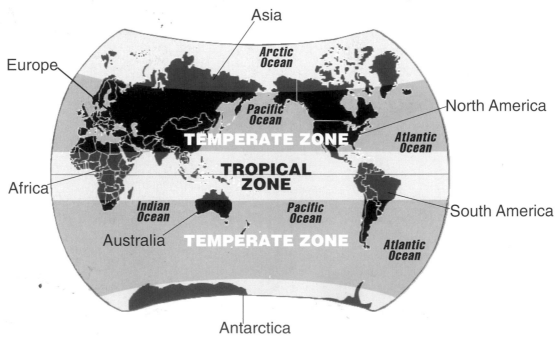

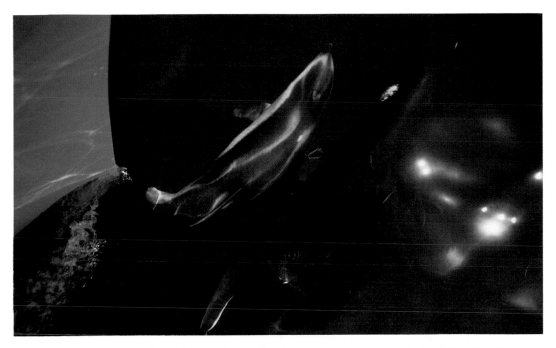

A Pacific white-sided dolphin and whale dolphin in the North Pacific Ocean.

Great Britain. The Pacific white-sided dolphins have different groups in the Northeast Pacific, Northwest Pacific, and Baja California.

When these dolphins are close to shore, they form **pods** of up to 40 members. **Herds** of over 1,000 members are found in open water. White-sided dolphins **migrate** to follow food.

SENSES

White-sided dolphins and people have 4 of the same senses. Their eyesight is good and they can see well in or out of the water. They are active dolphins and will often leap above the water and look around.

Hearing is their most important sense. Toothed whales have **echolocation**. By making a series of clicks and whistles, these dolphins can "see" underwater by listening to the returning echoes.

HOW ECHOLOCATION WORKS

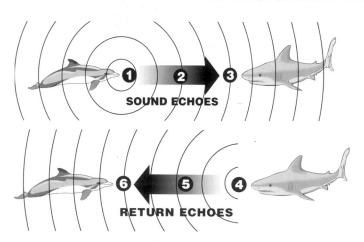

SOUND ECHOES

RETURN ECHOES

The dolphin sends out sound echoes (1). These echoes travel in all directions through the water (2). The sound echoes reach an object in the dolphin's path (3), then bounce off it (4). The return echoes travel through the water (5) and reach the dolphin (6). These echoes let the dolphin know where the object is, how large it is, and how fast it is moving.

White-sided dolphins are active. They will often leap above the water and look around.

White-sided dolphins are **social** animals. They often touch each other to **communicate**. They also have a sense of taste, but lack the sense of smell.

DEFENSE

Large sharks and killer whales will feed upon white-sided dolphins. Speed and quickness are their best defenses. Their well-developed sense of hearing allows the **pods** and **herds** to listen for danger and **communicate** warnings. Young dolphins and weak adults are the most likely **prey** because they cannot easily escape danger.

*White-sided dolphins swim with great
speed and quickness.*

FOOD

White-sided dolphins feed on different fish and **squid**. They find their **prey** with **echolocation**.

Atlantic white-sided dolphins have 28 to 40 pairs of small, sharp teeth per jaw. The Pacific white-sided dolphins have 21 to 33 pairs of slightly curved pointy teeth per jaw. These teeth are made to grab prey, not cut or chew.

White-sided dolphins work together to catch food. They also use loud clicks and whistles that can be heard long distances underwater.

The Pacific white-sided dolphin has 21 to 33 pairs of slightly curved, pointy teeth per jaw.

BABIES

A baby white-sided dolphin is called a **calf**. At birth, a calf is 2.5 to 3.5 feet (76 to 107 cm) long. Like other **mammals**, the mother makes milk for her calf.

White-sided dolphins are **social** animals. Females in the **pod** are related to the mother. These females will "baby-sit" the calf while the mother is feeding. This helps them to safely raise their calves. The calf will **nurse** for at least a year.

Female white-sided dolphins will establish a pod to baby-sit the calves.

WHITE-SIDED DOLPHIN FACTS

Scientific Name:

Atlantic white-sided dolphin *Lagenorhynchus acutus*

Pacific white-sided dolphin *L. obliquidens*

Average Size:

- 9 feet (2.7 meters)—Atlantic white-sided dolphin
- 7.5 feet (2.3 meters)—Pacific white-sided dolphin

Some Pacific groups are smaller. Males are generally larger than females.

Where They're Found: In the North Atlantic and North Pacific oceans in **sub-polar** and **temperate** waters.

A white-sided dolphin.

GLOSSARY

BOW WAVES - Water pushed up by the front of a ship.

CALF - A baby dolphin.

COMMUNICATE (kuh-MEW-nih-kate) - To show feelings.

DORSAL (DOOR-sull) - The fin on the back of a dolphin.

ECHOLOCATION (ek-oh-low-KAY-shun) - The use of sound waves to find objects underwater.

FLIPPERS - The forelimbs of a sea mammal.

FLUKES - The two lobes of a whale's tail.

HERD - A group of animals of one kind.

MAMMAL (MAM-ul) - A group of animals, including humans, that have hair and feed their young milk.

MIGRATE - To pass periodically from place to place repeatedly.

NURSE - To feed a child or young animal from its mother's breasts.

POD - A herd or school of sea mammals.

PREY - Animals that are eaten by other animals.

SNOUT - The part of an animal's head that projects forward and includes the nose, mouth, and jaws.

SOCIAL - To live in organized groups.

SPECIES (SPEE-seas) - A plant or animal belonging to a particular classification.

SQUID - Sea animals related to the octopus that are streamlined in shape and have at least ten arms.

SUB-POLAR - The cold area of Earth bordering the polar areas.

TEMPERATE (TEM-prit) - The part of the Earth where the oceans are not very hot, or not very cold.

WARM BLOODED - An animal whose body temperature remains the same and warmer than the outside air or water temperature.

Index

BIBLIOGRAPHY

Cousteau, Jacques-Yves. *The Whale, Mighty Monarch of the Sea.* N.Y.: Doubleday, 1972.

Dozier, Thomas A. *Whales and Other Sea Mammals.* Time-Life Films, 1977.

Leatherwood, Stephen. *The Sierra Club Handbook of Whales and Dolphins.* San Francisco, California: Sierra Club Books, 1983.

Minasian, Stanley M. *The World's Whales.* Washington, D.C.: Smithsonian Books, 1984.

Ridgway, Sam H., ed. *Mammals of the Sea.* Springfield, Illinois: Charles C. Thomas Publisher, 1972.